THE LITTLE BOOK OF
NEW ZEALAND RUGBY

Published by OH!
20 Mortimer Street
London W1T 3JW

ISBN 978-1-80069-063-9

Compiled by: Jamie Wall
Editorial: Lisa Dyer
Project manager: Russell Porter
Design: Andy Jones
Production: Freencky Portas

A CIP catalogue record for this book is available from the British Library

Printed in China

10 9 8 7 6 5 4 3 2 1

Jacket image: Freepik.com

THE LITTLE BOOK OF
NEW ZEALAND RUGBY

GENERAL EDITOR
JAMIE WALL

CONTENTS

INTRODUCTION

It's been said that *'the blackness of the jersey sends a shudder through your heart'*. The All Blacks are the team that defines excellence in the sport of rugby union, with an unmatched win record that sets them apart from everyone else. For almost 140 years, the team that represents New Zealand has stepped out onto fields across the world with a burning desire to win and enhance the legacy of those who have gone before them.

The All Blacks have been crowned official world champions three times; however, they had dominated the game long before the World Cup came into existence in 1987. The development of rugby as the national game of New Zealand meant that the fittest, most skillful and best athletes in the country have gravitated to rugby and the honour of wearing an All Black jersey. The dream of one day being an All Black is one held by every player in New Zealand, but only the absolute best are picked to perform the famous haka and be part of an enduring sporting story.

The All Blacks have helped spread the gospel of rugby around the world, with many entertaining tours and series against the world's leading nations, yet they have also forged a reputation for extremely tough play when required. There have been legendary rivalries with South Africa, the British & Irish Lions, Australia and France, and the team packs out stadiums around the world.

This concise little book tells the story of how the team came to be such a powerful force, in the words of the men who played both for and against the All Blacks. Legendary names of rugby tell their stories of being on the field and doing battle. Of wins, losses and how players are moulded to the New Zealand style of game. Of skills, determination and what it takes to be the best in the world.

Chapter
1

· · · · · · · ·

THE HISTORY

Rugby union is ingrained in
New Zealand culture as its national
game. The story of how it came to be
that way is key to the All Black story,
as is the rapid rise of the team in its
early days. The 1905 'Originals' and the
1924 'Invincibles' touring sides paved
the way for the future.

" Now some player runs with it,
and a general scrimmage ensues; it is all
shove, pull, rush and roll about in a confused
mass till 'down' is cried, and away the ball
goes again till perchance it gets in touch
or caught. **"**

*A slightly confused account of what is generally regarded
to be the first rugby union game played in New Zealand,
The Nelson Examiner, 1870*

❝ Sides were chosen…and some brisk play began, which however was scarcely according to the rules, only about six of those present knowing them. **❞**

Things were getting a little better a year later in the first inter-provincial game in Wellington, The Evening Post, *1871*

❝ How we did enjoy ourselves, both victors and vanquished, and how little we thought in those remote times that football would become the great national game of the colony… **❞**

Charles Monro

Organiser of the first inter-provincial game, 1871

❝ He could take his place in the front of a scrummage, and hook the ball with the best of them; his tremendous strength enabled him to burst through a pack, and then, when he was clear of the wreckage, and was well in the open, he was a perfect demon. **❞**

A Sydney writer describes Tom Ellison, the man who decreed that New Zealand rugby teams would play in black jerseys

1882

The first year that a New Zealand representative rugby union team played, against New South Wales. It would be another decade until they wore black jerseys, and another 23 years before they became known as the 'All Blacks'.

❝ The backs, or more particularly the five eighths, often ran with a directness that our players, who had a strange tendency to make for touch rather than the goal line, might take to heart; and when the moment made for a concerted movement, the men raced away at great pace, passing with a precision that was paralysing. **❞**

Daily Telegraph *describes the New Zealand team, 1905*

The 1905 tour stands as one of the nation's defining moments, as the country isolated in the South Pacific asserted itself on the world stage, proving they were about more than simply frozen lamb.

Tom Weir

British sports historian

❝ Every man took the field at Exeter keen and determined, yet cool and confident. **❞**

Billy Stead

On the team's opening match of the 1905 tour against Devon. While Devon were the current English champions, the All Blacks won 55–4

❝ It was a try, you know. ❞

Bob Deans

*His dying words at age 24, lamenting the disallowed try against Wales in 1905
that cost the Original All Blacks a perfect tour record*

❝ Its relevance is so real for every generation. Certainly in terms of the All Black folklore, the story stands out. It will remain a very defining aspect of the All Black story. The ultimate sacrifice they paid speaks to the importance of the jersey and everything it embodies. **❞**

Sir Michael Jones

The former All Black on the 100th anniversary of the
Battle of Passchendaele, the World War I engagement where
the Original All Black captain Dave Gallaher fell

14 MONTHS

The length of the 1888–89
New Zealand Natives' tour,
known as the forerunners to
the All Blacks. The team played
107 matches on their journey to
the UK, paving the way for future
rugby tours of all nations.

❝ Kings of Rugby – The papers are full of Sunday's match and unanimousely extol the All Blacks' magnificent game. The gate money is estimated at half a million francs, beating all records. ❞

As printed in Le Journal *newspaper, Paris, 13 January 1925*

" You have to understand, New Zealand is a very young country and rugby has put this country on the map. This country earned respect from the rest of the world for three things: what we did in two world wars, and to a lesser extent what we've done on the rugby field. So over time rugby has become a major part of our national identity. **"**

Sir Graham Henry

World Cup-winning All Black coach

" The crucial thing there was the 1905 All Black team. The context of that was that New Zealand had always – has always – had a certain insecurity about its place in the world. We've always got a certain anxiety that we are falling off the edge, that we don't really count. **"**

Jock Phillips

Historian

❝ In New Zealand it was truly a classless game, the butchers boy would play and fraternise with the local doctor, the town youths would play with the policeman. **❞**

Alan Turley
Rugby historian

❝ There's no yielding to status in a rugby tackle, there's no privilege in a scrum. **❞**

Sir Richard Wild

Chief Justice of New Zealand, 1967

246

Billy Wallace scored this total
number of points on the 1905
All Black tour to the UK, made
all the more impressive given
the relatively low-scoring nature
of the game at the time.

❝ Nobody expects the All Blacks to do so well in 1924 as they did in 1905. Rugby in Britain has improved considerably since the latter year, while it is questionable that New Zealand form is as good as it was then. **❞**

The Evening Post, 1924. The team went on to win all 38 of its matches in the UK, France and North America, becoming known as the 'Invincibles'.

Chapter

2

• • • • • • • •

HOW AN ALL BLACK IS MADE

The process of pulling on a black jersey starts at a young age in New Zealand. Junior clubs and school rugby are vital for the development of players, as is the inclusive nature of the game. This ethos is how the competition among all grades remains strong.

❝ The key to New Zealand rugby is the strength of the competitions our young people play. Especially in the schools. **❞**

Sir Graham Henry

World Cup-winning All Black coach

" Because I was the first of the modern breed to not only make the All Blacks but stay in there for some time. And what started as a trickle became a flood. I was followed by lots of young Polynesians, second, third generation, people brought up here in New Zealand. **"**

Sir Bryan Williams

All Black and second-generation Samoan-New Zealander

" You have got people working together, coordinating the development of players through the schools system, to their provincial rugby, right through to the All Blacks. There is a big emphasis on skill, and less on tactics, especially in the teenage years. It is a totally integrated system. **"**

Sir Ian McGeechan
British & Irish Lions coach

❝ Boys have had to fight for everything they've got, but they've matured later, and they're not burned out and they're not over-coached. **❞**

Danny Port
Christchurch Boys High School coach

52

The most All Blacks to date produced by one school, Auckland Grammar. Christchurch Boys High School is next with 46, followed by Wellington College with 35.

❝ We could not help noticing the fine state of fitness in which every man appeared to take the field. Teams in New Zealand are in much better training than at home…it is evident that much more attention is given to preparation than in the Old Country. **❞**

A. F. Harding

British & Irish Lions captain, 1904

“ We will always recall the complete disregard for self with which a New Zealand forward charges the line – almost as if there were no one to stand in his path. **”**

Ginger Osborne

British & Irish Lions manager, 1950

❝ We all think to some extent you people are quite mad. Though we may laugh and joke about it, we cannot fail to be impressed by the effect a simple game like rugby has upon a country like yours. **❞**

Alf Wilson
British & Irish Lions player, 1959

❝ The gas station owner says there is a steady trickle of tourists who come to see the Carters' house. Dan's parents once came home and found a Japanese family having a picnic on their lawn, underneath the goalposts. **❞**

Andy Bull

Writing in The Guardian *on Dan Carter's family home in Southbridge, where his father constructed his own set of post*

❝ When I first played for Taranaki in '86, we played for the love of it. And most of us, if not all of us, were farmers. So we would get up at 4.30 in the morning to milk the cows, do a day's work, and then go training. Same on game day. **❞**

Kevin 'Smiley' Barrett

Taranaki stalwart

520

The number of rugby clubs
in New Zealand.

❝ The big thing was taking enough drink to get through the day, and then be able to run home with all this gear. So that work was part of our training. You were working like bloody hell. We used to pray for the rugby season to come round, because it meant we could knock off early to go training. **❞**

Sir Colin Meads

All Black captain

" There are gold nuggets in every school. We've got to try and get them out of the earth, and grab them and polish them and make them into gold coins. **"**

Ian Parata

Bay of Plenty Secondary Schools rugby manager

" This is a dream come true. Growing up as a kid in New Zealand, you always wanted to be an All Black so this is very special. Today is Father's Day so it's probably the best gift I've given my dad. I told my parents and they burst into tears, I couldn't hear what they were saying but there were tears. **"**

Tupou Vaa'i

Newly capped 2020 All Black

❝ At 12 or 13 I wanted to make the most out of every opportunity and not have any regrets. Habits such as working hard and setting your sights pretty high – that's what I've done for so long. **❞**

Richie McCaw

Record-holding All Black captain

❝ I went into Tewie's office and said [no matter] how much he costs, just get him. This kid's special. **❞**

Steve Hansen

*World Cup-winning All Black coach to Steve Tew
(then Canterbury CEO), on Richie McCaw*

" Suddenly your mates are there, not just over the ball but over you, protecting you. They're prepared to put their bodies on the line for you. That's what happens in life: you fall over and your mates come to your aid. **"**

Sir John Kirwan
All Black winger

66 I began competitive football at 12, playing in an under-18 grade. This was a tough way to begin winning your way. It's one thing to be big for your age, but to put a 12-year-old against rugged, work-hardened farm boys was a big thing. **99**

Don Clarke
All Black fullback

46

The amount of sets of brothers who have played for the All Blacks, including the Whetton twins (Gary and AJ) and three Barrett brothers (Beauden, Scott and Jordie).

❝ Farming has been all we know. Not farming of the country-squire kind. Farming of the work-till-you-drop-or-you-go-under kind. **❞**

Zinzan Brooke

All Black number eight

“ Memories of those early days of rugby are just the sheer thrill of playing, of accepting that I had natural-born skills with the ball and taking every opportunity to show them off. **”**

Zinzan Brooke

All Black number eight

❝ Sport was everything to me. I would much rather be outside running about and kicking a ball than sitting inside on the gaming console...it got me outside where I could enjoy the number-one privilege of so many New Zealand kids: the freedom to roam. **❞**

Kieran Read

All Black captain

" The thing you've got to remember about the New Zealanders is that they are unbelievably innovative and have this capacity to reinvent the way they play the game all the time, so that they are always streets ahead of everyone else. **"**

Ian McLaughlan

Scotland and British & Irish Lions prop

❝ My eyes were wide as saucers that week and my mind devoured everything that was thrown at it...by the time the game arrived I was living attack structures and set moves... **❞**

Kieran Read

The future All Black captain, on being selected for the
New Zealand Secondary Schools team

Chapter

3

• • • • • • •

WHAT THE JERSEY MEANS

To represent the All Blacks means more
than just playing a game of rugby.
The weight of a nation's expectations
ride on every time they take the field,
and this is not lost on the men that have
to perform week in and week out.

" Son, you've got to be prepared to piss blood to wear this jersey. **"**

Mark 'Cowboy' Shaw

All Black flanker, to debutant Mike Brewer, 1986

❝ Scholars have written books about it and, as the undisputed best team on the planet, you can toss around words like 'legacy' without fear of contradiction. **❞**

Dylan Cleaver

The New Zealand Herald

❝ We don't understand how good we are, how great we are in this game of rugby… we've won, historically, about 75 per cent of our games, which is huge in the international sporting arena – yet we lose a couple of tests and all of a sudden the world has come to an end. **❞**

John Hart
All Black coach

❝ A persistent finger injury incurred from playing as a softball catcher put Red Conway's 1960 tour of South Africa in doubt…after the break mended, the finger retained a kink and he was told by a specialist that if he kept playing rugby the finger would keep breaking. To keep his spot on the tour, Conway decided to amputate the finger after the final selection trial. **❞**

New Zealand Rugby Archives

❝ I'd never known a nation to take defeat like it…and I was saying, 'Well, yeah, but it's a game. You've got your family and you've got your health.' And they'd say, 'It isn't a game, it's everything.' They were pointing to the silver fern and crying, grown men. **❞**

Phil Bennett

Commenting after the All Blacks 1999 Rugby World Cup semifinal loss

" Rugby was my life…I came to play in every game of the tour – 38 matches, playing twice a week for four months at fullback. No other player, I have been told, has ever done this on a long tour. "

George Nepia

All Black fullback on the Invincibles' tour

78 percent

The All Blacks' win record since their first official test in 1903. The next highest among any test team is the Springboks, with 63 percent.

❝ It is not a fear of losing; it's a fear of letting your country down. **❞**

Sir Colin Meads

All Black captain

There's four million New Zealanders, who have all got a view about what's right and what's wrong.

Brent Anderson

Former All Black player and commentator

❝ This is what I said to them: 'Rugby is special, you put a jersey on and play for your province, or get picked for your country and pull on the All Black jersey, that's a huge honour. But always remember who you are and where you came from, and always keep your feet on the ground. Because the day you take your jersey off you're just one of us.' **❞**

Kevin 'Smiley' Barrett

Talking to his All Black sons, Beauden, Scott and Jordie

❝ You don't get a lot of time in the jersey, so you have to cherish every moment you have. It's about doing the best you can when you pull the jersey on. **❞**

Aaron Mauger
All Black midfielder

❝ I don't believe in magic. I believe
in hard work. **❞**

Richie McCaw

Record-holding All Black captain

“ The legacy is more intimidating than any opposition. **”**

Sean Fitzpatrick
All Black captain

" They mostly win but they always, or nearly always, turn up with an internal sense of fear driving them into collisions harder than their opponents. **"**

Gregor Paul

The New Zealand Herald

9

The amount of tries scored
by the All Blacks in World Cup
final matches.

❝ The final decision to retire came after my last game in 2015, but there was plenty of thought that went into it, especially throughout my final year. I could never get enough of the thrill of pulling on the jersey and running out in front of thousands of people, and that is what I will always miss. **❞**

Richie McCaw

Record-holding All Black captain

❝ At the end of the game I got a tap on the shoulder, it was my brother Ross and he said, 'There's an old bugger up in the stand wants to see you,' so I went up and saw Dad. Just seeing the look on his face, I was in tears, he was so proud. I remembered that when I saw my son Tom played for the All Blacks. I knew how my Dad felt. **❞**

Warwick Taylor
World Cup-winning All Black

❝ You're always striving for the perfect game. For me, that was probably the closest I got in my 112 Test matches for the All Blacks. You'll never say that you've played the perfect game... but that was as close as I got. **❞**

Dan Carter

The world-record-holding points scorer on his
33-point performance against the Lions in 2005

❝ He was a fabulous role model for everybody because he epitomised what we were trying to achieve; humble guys all striving to get better. He coined the phrase 'Better people make better All Blacks', and he lived that. **❞**

Sir Graham Henry

On fellow World Cup-winning coach Sir Brian Lochore

If you know anything about rugby at least you know about the All Blacks, and I always knew about them.

Rhett Ellison

NFL player and descendent of Tom Ellison

❝ The All Blacks have been incredibly consistent for what seems like forever but all the rest of them, there's no guarantee that any of the other teams beat New Zealand on any given day. **❞**

Martin Johnson
England captain

❝ I pride myself on not copying other teams, but I loved their little saying which underpins recent great New Zealand sides, namely 'no dickheads'. It's pretty self-explanatory. **❞**

Sir Clive Woodward

England coach

❝ I am shattered, our dreams are shattered and I feel sick about it all. **❞**

John Hart

All Black coach, after the All Blacks' World Cup semifinal loss in 1999

" It wasn't until after the final whistle when I had all this joy, and I just loved this feeling of standing out on Eden Park with my teammates feeling so happy, and then I realized this was going to be the last time that I get to experience this feeling in New Zealand. It was quite sad, I didn't want that feeling to end. **"**

Dan Carter

After winning the World Cup in 2015

61,240

The record attendance for an
All Black test in New Zealand,
at Eden Park in 1956. Auckland's
population at the time was
around 300,000.

" Yup, I played rugby as a kid when I lived in New Zealand. Toughest sport I've ever done. #Respect. **"**

Dwayne 'The Rock' Johnson

Pro wrestler and Hollywood icon on Twitter

❝ It is one of the greatest presents I have ever been given. I never leave home without it. It always travels with me. **❞**

Jason Momoa

Aquaman *and* Game of Thrones *star on his prized All Black jersey, a gift from a close friend*

❝ I admire the boys that went because that's the sort of thing I would have done. I wouldn't have gone to assembly in the morning. I would have made sure I was there. It was a great occasion and a great opportunity to see their heroes. **❞**

Sir Colin Meads

On high school students who skipped class
to attend the 2011 World Cup parade

‟ This will be one hell of a team, but it won't be playing the type of football you're used to seeing. This team will run with the ball at every opportunity and it will win by scoring tries – not by kicking goals. **”**

Fred Allen

All Black coach, 1967

❝ Every day, we get up to be the best in the world. **❞**

Jock Hobbs

All Black and New Zealand Rugby administrator

Chapter

4

• • • • • • • •

THE HAKA

The famous pre-match ritual of the
All Blacks is a powerful insight into the
Māori culture of New Zealand, and its
importance to the nation.
Often misunderstood as a threatening
gesture, the haka is more of a way of
honouring opponents and drawing
strength. The All Blacks currently
perform either the traditional 'Ka Mate'
haka or the newer 'Kapa o Pango'
before every test match.

" People think it is a war challenge, but to be honest mate, we never came to the battlefield to tell you that we were here to challenge you. We came to kill you. The haka isn't about the enemy. It is about us. It's about opening ourselves up to our ancestors, to their spirits, about filling ourselves with their strengths and gifts. It is hard to explain. And to be honest, most Europeans don't get it. **"**

Tiki Edwards

New Zealand Rugby community manager

" The true value of the haka is in connection, and as the opposition, you need to decide how you are going to connect and not dissipate as a team in that moment. **"**

John Eales

Former Wallabies captain

❝ Some guys at my rugby club, Ottawa Irish, said if you want to learn how to play rugby, watch the All Blacks, so I did and I was mesmerised by how good they were, and by the haka and everything else. **❞**

Al Charron
Canadian test player

❝ It's about understanding the culture.
It's about us reuniting with our past. **❞**

Steve Hansen

All Black coach

" Facing the haka is a couple of minutes, but it's a couple of minutes you'll always remember. **"**

Jacques Burger

Namibian captain

❝ Whether you are Māori, Samoan or European, it doesn't matter where you are from. When you are an All Black, you are united as one, and we show this through performing the haka. **❞**

Dan Carter
All Black player

1987

The year that the All Blacks started performing the haka regularly on New Zealand soil. Before then, it had been mostly done for tours overseas.

❝ The enduring power of the haka is its ability to connect the team within each other, and also with their heritage, history and their country. **❞**

John Eales

Former Wallabies captain

" At the time, you're extremely proud, a little emotional, and you ask yourself, 'How did I end up doing this?' **"**

Greg Feek

All Black player

❝ But you could sense the crowd feeling it. It gave us a big lift right just before we went out and laid it all on the line. It pushed us even further. **❞**

Conor Murray

Irish test player on his team's iconic response to the haka before Ireland's first-ever win over the All Blacks in 2016

❝ You have to not only match them in the haka, you have to go toe to toe the whole way. In fairness, it was Jimmy Davidson's idea and I suppose he got a few…idiotic lieutenants to carry it out. And the atmosphere was…if you could have bottled it, you would have made a fortune. **❞**

Willie Anderson

Irish captain on their confrontational haka response in 1989

" I think their was response was fantastic...If you understand the haka, the haka requires a response. It's a challenge to you personally...so I thought it was brilliant and imaginative. **"**

Steve Hansen

On the England team's 2019 haka response

❝ It was necessary to calm them down. But it's a great moment we'll all remember. I felt during the week that the players wanted to do something during the haka, like they did in 2007. **❞**

Thierry Dusautoir

The French captain on their unified march towards the haka at the 2011 Rugby World Cup final

❝ It was all about making sure we didn't embarrass ourselves in front of the world and in front of our own Māori people. We got it right, though, and the haka has just grown exponentially from there. **❞**

Buck Shelford

*All Black captain and the man credited with reviving
what the haka meant in the 1980s*

20 metres

The supposed distance World Rugby had mandated that the two teams keep apart during the haka. This is, however, routinely ignored.

❝ They welcomed the Blackheath men with the old chant which representative teams in New Zealand have long since made their own, beginning 'Ka mate, ka mate! Ka ora, ka ora' and ending in a fearsome yell. Their war-cry was terrible, but it was not so full of terrors as their play. **❞**

A report on the haka and subsequent game by the Daily Telegraph *in 1905*

“ The association between rugby and haka has a rich history spanning more than 130 years. Since the New Zealand Natives team first performed haka during their tour of Britain in 1888–89, haka has endured and grown across all of rugby. **”**

Luke Crawford

New Zealand Rugby kaumātua (Māori cultural leader)

❝ You look back at certain things
in your life and think, 'Oh, I wish
I didn't do that'. **❞**

John Eales

On his team's infamous decision to turn their backs on the haka in 1996,
after which they were thrashed 43–6

❝ Playing the All Blacks, you can't wait. They're the best team in the world. You need to attack them right from the start. **❞**

Manu Tuilagi

On England's v-shaped haka tactic before their
2019 Rugby World Cup semifinal win

❝ It was an enormous honour, one that was widely depicted as an act of defiance on my part. That couldn't be further from the truth. I had a team that was hurting, one that needed to make one final push for the year. I wasn't trying to prove anything to the public. I was standing in front of my men and leading them. **❞**

Kieran Read

All Blacks captain on leading the haka

&& Even for Māori back home to see non-Māori go through the processes to learn why he's leading haka, pronouncing the words the right way, and doing it the way he's performed it, that's special to me, not even as a rugby player or a teammate, but as a Māori. **§§**

TJ Perenara

All Black halfback on Read's decision to lead

❝ Hopefully the Poms keep complaining about the advantage the haka gives the All Blacks. It's great, it's just fodder. **❞**

Gary Whetton
All Black player

The original 'Ka Mate' haka has nothing to do with rugby. It was composed around 1820 by Te Rauparaha, a rangatira (chief) and war leader of the Ngāti Toa iwi (tribe), after he had successfully escaped from his enemies.

It is unknown as to how it became the favoured haka for the All Blacks later on.

❝ We talked over a lot of aspects of the haka, about what it means to some of the new players and its effectiveness. We all left there with a greater insight into the haka and how it brought us all together – all the different cultures we have within the All Blacks. **❞**

Tana Umaga

All Black captain on the new Kapa o Pango haka in 2005

❝ It's a challenge, they want to smash you, you want to smash them, alright you want to take this on, let's have a crack. ❞

Richard Cockerill

The English hooker's feelings on the haka, 1997

" I can feel their fighting spirit. When we line up and we are watching the All Blacks perform the haka, it makes me think to myself, 'we can do it!' **"**

Shota Horie

Japanese player

ff I used to sit in a corner. I didn't change until 30 minutes before the game. The haka was my warmup. **JJ**

Sir Colin Meads

All Black captain

‟ We're f**ked. **”**

Nathan Sharpe

Wallaby captain to no one in particular, after the bolt of lightning and crack of
thunder coincided with the climax of the haka at Eden Park, 2008.
The All Blacks went on to win 39–10.

Chapter

5

· · · · · · · ·

FAMOUS
VICTORIES

The All Blacks have had many
memorable matches over the years,
including three World Cup final wins,
a series win in South Africa and a
dominant record against the British &
Irish Lions. They play annually for the
Bledisloe Cup against Australia, and
have won the Rugby Championship
16 out of the 24 times it has been held.

❝ They hung on, history was made and my 15 minutes against the All Blacks was not one of fame, but pain. **❞**

James Dalton

Springbok hooker after the All Blacks' epic 1996 series win in South Africa

" The All Blacks that day looked like great
prophets of doom. **"**

Bill McLaren

Legendary Scottish commentator

❝ I'd rather die than go through that experience again. **❞**

Mike Campbell-Lamerton

British & Irish Lions captain after first test loss in 1966

" It's time we stopped kidding ourselves about the standard of rugby in the Five Nations. You could not have a more dedicated, committed team than these Lions but they were not good enough – they were lambs to the slaughter. "

Jim Telfer

Lions coach on his side's 0–4 series defeat in 1983

❝ The New Zealanders are the men of the moment. Their visit has shaken up the dry bones of rugby football and created a revival in the game that will be felt for years to come. **❞**

A Limerick newspaper on the All Blacks' win over Ireland in 1905

“ We improved a bit as we went on our way, it just flowed along like a river. **”**

George Gillett

All Black player, 1905

Sydney

The city in which the All Blacks have played their most games isn't even in New Zealand. Sydney has hosted the team over 100 times in both test and tour matches, with the vast majority of games against Australia and New South Wales in the early years held in Australia's largest city.

❝ What I remember most is the intensity of preparation. There was a fervour to beat the Boks for the first time in a series. It was almost a win-at-all-costs mentality. **❞**

Pat Vincent

All Black captain on the 1956 series against South Africa

❝ The team talk [before the fourth test] was given in the Commercial Room of the Station Hotel. It was the greatest team talk imaginable. Tom Morrison told us there were sixty thousand people out there at the park waiting and hoping for the first victory in 62 years and we must not let them down. That was about all he had to say. A man's nerves were at a high pitch, the countdown was starting. **❞**

Peter Jones

All Black flanker before the fourth test in 1956

❝ I'm absolutely buggered. **❞**

Peter Jones

After the fourth test in 1956, won by the All Blacks
after Jones scored a crucial second-half try

❝ If you're playing well and kicking well there's nothing that can't be accomplished… when I went to take that kick, that final kick, I felt as confident as anything and said to myself, 'I'll get this one'. **❞**

Don Clarke

On a crucial sideline conversion against the Springboks in 1960

❝ South Africa do target top players to get rid of them. There are no easy games in South Africa for the boys. **❞**

Fergie McCormick

All Black fullback

" When I scored the try and got up the crowd was going bananas, I felt bloody embarrassed…I was walking back and thought if there was a hole I could jump into I would. **"**

Ian Kirkpatrick

All Black flanker on his iconic try from halfway against the Lions in 1971

❝ Touring was a different story in those days. You just turned up in your training gear. There was no meeting to talk about how difficult it was going to be being away for four months, difficulties at home, the financial problems guys were having to go through, there was none of that. **❞**

Ian Kirkpatrick
All Black flanker, 1973

15

The amount of World Cup tries scored by the great Jonah Lomu. After the 1995 tournament, it was his starring role that hastened the game's move to professionalism, due to eager offers from competing broadcasters.

❝ As soon as I hit it, I knew from the way it felt on my boot that I had kicked the goal. I started turning back before the touch judges had raised their flags. **❞**

Brian McKechnie

Double international (he also played international cricket for New Zealand) on his controversial penalty goal against Wales in 1978 that sealed a 13–12 win on the All Blacks' Grand Slam tour

“ Oh Mr Haden,
these calls are for you. **”**

Cardiff hotel receptionist with a full switchboard to All Black lock Andy Haden,
after his infamous lineout dive that led to McKechnie's penalty

❝ I think there was a bit of a sea change in that test of how All Black teams played the game because it was very much a day where the team had no thought of losing. It was a case of 'Let's get out there and be the best we can be. We know we're better than these guys…' **❞**

Graham Mourie

All Black captain on the 1980 test win against Wales

“ Someone was going, 'Don't think about the plane, take the plane out of the equation,' and I'm thinking, 'Don't think about the plane?' I can see the colour of the guy's eyes. **”**

Stu Wilson

All Black winger on the 'Flour Bomb Test' against South Africa in 1981,
which saw a light plane flown by anti-apartheid protesters
drop debris on the field for the duration of the game

❝ He said, 'You've got two choices, you can either be here for a weekend and think you've arrived, or you can be here ten years and think you've never arrived.' That formed my attitude to the All Blacks very early. **❞**

Sir John Kirwan

On advice he received in 1984

❝ All of a sudden as a 22-year-old I was
playing alongside some of the best
All Blacks that were ever to grace the field.
Not only that, they were at the top of their
game. It couldn't have been better. **❞**

Sir Michael Jones

On the 1987 Rugby World Cup campaign

" We were never going to lose.
There was a determination among all
of us that was fantastically palpable and
great to be part of. **"**

Sir John Kirwan
All Black winger, 1987

The heaviest recorded All Black is 136 kilogram (300lb) Neemia Tialata, who played between 2005 and 2010.

The lightest is Alan 'Ponty' Reid, who clocked in at 59 kilograms (130lb) in his career between 1951–57.

❝ I raised my fist to the crowd to say, 'We've won!', and they just erupted in unison. Going up the steps in the Eden Park grandstand to receive the Cup was a great buzz. But a sense of relief as well. **❞**

Murray Pierce

All Black lock after the All Blacks had won the Rugby World Cup

❝ I had a beer with le Roux afterwards, and then he got banned for 18 months. **❞**

Sean Fitzpatrick

Reflecting on the All Blacks' 13–9 win over the Springboks in 1994, in which he infamously had his ear bitten by Springbok prop Johan le Roux

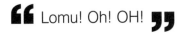 Lomu! Oh! OH!

Keith Quinn

Commentator on Jonah Lomu's first of four tries in the
1995 Rugby World Cup semifinal against England

❝ You can't really express how amazing it felt. It was a great occasion and I'm glad we could share it with the people of New Zealand. **❞**

Piri Weepu

All Black halfback on the 2011 Rugby World Cup win

" Yes, I am eating humble pie.
I would just like to congratulate the
All Blacks again. **"**

David Campese
Former Australian winger in 2020, after he claimed the All Blacks' aura of
invincibility 'as gone'. That weekend the All Blacks defeated the
Wallabies 43–5, a record scoreline.

Chapter
6
• • • • • • •
GREAT PLAYERS

The All Blacks have produced some of the brightest stars in the game over their history. These men have played their parts in making rugby union one of the biggest sports in the world and are household names in New Zealand. Not only have they left their mark on the All Blacks, but also brought out the best in their legendary opponents as well.

" With Richie McCaw, Dan Carter or Kieran Read, now what they give to the younger players is invaluable. Seeing how they train and how they approach each week that is the kind of thing you want to carry on; to see the values and what it means. **"**

Victor Matfield

Springbok player, 2016

❝ The only way really for any team to stand a chance is to put them under pressure – eliminate space and eliminate time. There are only two ways to do that; you got to have a very fast and aggressive defence or be brave and don't give them the ball. **❞**

John Smit
Springbok captain

66 Every time he would get hold of Keven, Keven would just get angrier and angrier and more of a threat. Eventually, after the third time, I said to Bakkies, 'Stop everything you are doing with this guy. The more you are irritating him, the better he is getting.' **99**

John Smit

On All Black test centurion Keven Mealamu

❝ There was real excitement and tension –
maybe because we had such a low win ratio
against them – and as players we lived off
that energy. That spurred us on. I had a lot
of friends and family there, and it is a
memory that will stay with me for
the rest of my life. **❞**

Chris Robshaw
England captain

" For South Africans, the ultimate is to play the All Blacks. **"**

Naas Botha
Springbok legend

❝ On that tour I think Fitzy got 186 stitches in the head, in the end I was stitching him – the doctor had had enough. **❞**

Sir John Kirwan

On the bloody aftermath of the 1986 tour of France

“ New Zealand is a very unforgiving environment and the '93 Lions' tour was tough. The second Test in Wellington, though, was special. **”**

Peter Winterbottom

England and Lions flanker

" Out-smashing the All Blacks is the only way we can beat the All Blacks. We can't out-run them. "

Bob Skinstad

Springbok captain

23

The amount of New Zealand
players, coaches, journalists and
teams that have been inducted
into the World Rugby Hall of Fame.

❝ You want to test yourself against the best…the All Blacks are the best. **❞**

Gareth Rees
Canadian captain

" Jonah was freakish, he was such a weapon…when we made space for him, those guys, poor Tony Underwood, Catt, Carling…they had no chance. **"**

Jeff Wilson

All Black winger on his teammate, Jonah Lomu

❝ I met Jonah Lomu. I never knew how huge he was. I felt like a peasant in a Godzilla movie: 'Quickly! Go tell the other villagers! We go now!' **❞**

Robin Williams

The acting great, on Jonah Lomu

❝ Remember that rugby is a team game. All 14 of you make sure you pass the ball to Jonah. **❞**

Fax received by the All Blacks, 1995

❝ That we will hear a lot in the future about the new openside Richie McCaw is the safest bet in modern rugby. **❞**

Rob Kitson

Writing about the future 148-cap All Black captain in 2001

" Wilson could be with the Queen and do it perfect. Then he could be with a drunken Welshman on the street and be perfect. **"**

Sir Colin Meads

All Black captain on Sir Wilson Whineray

" Colin Meads is the kind of player you expect to see emerging from a ruck with the remains of a jockstrap between his teeth. **"**

Tom O'Reilly
Author

" I went to the sideline, and the doc looked at it and said, 'I think you've just pinched a nerve.' Really? I'm not going off for a bloody pinched nerve. So I carried on playing. But I knew it wasn't right – there was something terribly wrong with it. I couldn't hold the prop. You know something's wrong when you can't move your hand. **"**

Sir Colin Meads

Reminiscing about continuing to play with a broken arm in 1970

❝ I was only ever operating at 80 percent of my capacity. **❞**

Jonah Lomu

On the kidney disease that afflicted him throughout his career.
It ultimately claimed his life at age 40.

66 A bloke who never sought greatness but who just wanted to be an All Black. **99**

Alex Veysey

Writer, on Colin Meads

" I'm no hod carrier but I'd be laying bricks if he was running at me. **"**

Bill McLaren

Rugby commentator on Jonah Lomu

❝ Here we had this huge man who was incredibly fast that all we needed to do was get the ball to him as quickly as possible without too many people out there marking him. The instructions for our backs were: just get the ball to Jonah as fast as you can and back him up. **❞**

Laurie Mains

All Black coach

❝ A favourite [tactic] of Fred's was to read out telegrams in the dressing room before matches, which he said came from supporters and that said things like: 'Meads is over the hill' and 'Meads has been there for too long'. He would do that to get you fired up and also show the youngsters that no one was above criticism. But of course he would have composed the telegrams himself. **❞**

Sir Colin Meads

All Black captain on coach Fred Allen

❝ Rugby is basically a running, passing game so our number-one priority will be to attack at all times from all parts of the field. **❞**

Fred Allen

Former All Black and coach

❝ It's something very special to play against New Zealand. The French team and All Blacks have a special history together and we're going to write a new chapter. I hope it will be a nice one for the French team. **❞**

Thierry Dusautoir

Before the 2015 World Cup quarter final.
The All Blacks won by a record score of 62–13.

1,477,294

The total number of spectators that attended the Rugby World Cup when it was held in New Zealand in 2011. That's an average of 30,777 per match.

** Unless you are prepared to work hard, you are going to get nothing. Whether it be rugby, or in any sport, you have to work hard or you are not going to get anywhere. **

Buck Shelford

All Black captain

❝ Given the legacy of the rivalry, we have a responsibility. I thought that I'd never go to South Africa as an All Black (because of isolation), let alone as a captain. And that's very special to me. **❞**

Sean Fitzpatrick

All Black captain

" You tend to remember when you play the All Blacks. **"**

Brian Moore

Tweet by England test player

“ You know what, Michael Hooper grabbed my nuts just then. **”**

Caleb Clarke

New All Black on his onfield experience at Eden Park in 2020

" Every time we play you blokes it's on, it's on from word go and thank you for inviting us in here, it's the other stuff in rugby that's quite special too. **"**

Michael Hooper

Wallaby captain, after the teams shared a beer in the sheds post-match, 2020

&& For England, it doesn't get any bigger than playing New Zealand for a place in the World Cup final – it's the stuff of dreams. **&&**

Matt Dawson

English halfback

" Australia opened up the doors to bring players back, it's the same in South Africa but there's so much depth in New Zealand rugby that they don't need players like me to come back. **"**

Dan Carter
All Black player

" If our blokes are on form, and the All Blacks are out of form, and the wind blows from the east and the rooster crows at dawn, we're in with half a sniff of half a chance! **"**

Peter FitzSimons

Former Wallaby and Australian journalist

❝ The first day I put on this jersey I just didn't want to let it down, I wanted to add to the legacy of what was 100 odd years before. **❞**

Richie McCaw

Record-holding All Black captain

Out of a combined 140 tests against the UK 'Home' unions, the All Blacks have won 123 times.

The last Welsh win came in 1953, while Scotland have never defeated the All Blacks in well over a century of trying.

66 I was never good enough to play for the All Blacks. I'd give up everything I've done in coaching to play one game. And most people would say I'd be lucky. **99**

Steve Hansen

World Cup winning All Black coach, 2015

❝ He was class, just so silky smooth the way he ran. It's very rewarding to lay a platform down and you've got those guys on the outside, you know they are going to do something with it. **❞**

Craig Dowd

All Black prop on Christian Cullen, 1996

“ We were driven by the challenge of
beating South Africa in South Africa and
making history. **”**

Sir Michael Jones

All Black player, 1996

❝ There'll be a moment when it comes down to one or decisions; one or two moments will be the difference between you going home and winning the thing. **❞**

Richie McCaw

Record-holding All Black captain, 2015

❝ It's an era people will look back on and say how lucky we were to see guys like Dan and Richie play. It has been a huge honour to play alongside them. **❞**

Jerome Kaino

All Black flanker

The highest-ever scorer for the
All Blacks is Dan Carter with
1598 points.

The highest try scorer is
Doug Howlett with 49.

The most capped is
Richie McCaw with 148.

❝ Sonny would be the best athlete I've coached from a pure athlete sense. He's a freak of nature. **❞**

Steve Hansen
On Sonny Bill Williams

❝ I aim for perfection, but I know that's not achievable so I'm always working to be better every day. **❞**

Beauden Barrett
All Black flyhalf

❝ I owe this game everything.
I love this sport, I love everything it's
given me. **❞**

Aaron Smith

All Black halfback

" It is the identity of the of the team that matters – not so much what the All Blacks do, but who they are, what they stand for, and why they exist. **"**

James Kerr

Author